D0482093

Other books in this series:
Golf Quotations
Teddy Bear Quotations
Horse Lover's Quotations
Book Lover's Quotations

Published in Great Britain in 1991 by
Exley Publications Ltd
16 Chalk Hill, Watford, Herts WD1 4BN, United Kingdom.
Paintings © Frank Archer
Selection and arrangement © Helen Exley 1991

ISBN 1-85015-267-5

EDITOR: HELEN EXLEY
Designed by Pinpoint Design Company
Printed and bound by Graficas Reunidas SA, Madrid, Spain

MUSIC
Lovers
QUOTATIONS

PAINTINGS BY FRANK ARCHER

EXLEY

PIERRE BOULEZ

"For the past eighty years I have started each day in the same manner. It is not a mechanical routine but something essential to my daily life. I go to the piano, and I play two preludes and fugues of Bach. I cannot think of doing otherwise. It is a sort of benediction on the house. But that is not its only meaning for me. It is a rediscovery of the world of which I have the joy of being a part. It fills me with awareness of the wonder of life, with a feeling of the incredible marvel of being a human being."

PABLO CASALS (1876 - 1973),
from *Joys and Sorrows*

"If I had my life to live over again, I would have made a rule to read some poetry and listen to some music at least once a week; for perhaps the parts of my brain now atrophied would thus have been kept active through use. The loss of these tastes is a loss of happiness, and may possibly be injurious to the intellect, and more probably to the moral character, by enfeebling the emotional part of our nature."

CHARLES DARWIN (1809 - 82)

"To keep young, every day read a poem, hear a choice piece of music, view a fine painting, and, if possible, do a good action. Man's highest merit always is, as much as possible, to rule external circumstances, and as little as possible to let himself be ruled by them."
JOHANN WOLFGANG VON GOETHE (1749 - 1832)

"Music is the fourth great material want of our natures, - first food, then raiment, then shelter, then music."
CHRISTIAN BOVÉE

MOZART CONCERTO (detail)

KIRI TE KANAWA

"To listen to Monteverdi's Vespers on a summer evening is to waken astonished to find oneself in the wrong century."
PAM BROWN, b.1928

"Through music we may wander where we will in time, and find friends in every century."
HELEN THOMSON

"We know an age more vividly through its music than its historians."
ROSANNE AMBROSE-BROWN

"Why speak of time travel? We have a tried and proven method with us. Music moves us across centuries and continents without ever leaving our chairs.
Today I have stood in the huge quietness of Solemnes, circled the glittering ballrooms of Vienna, walked in Pepys' Whitehall, careered about the room in the exuberance of a Victorian polka."
PAM BROWN, b.1928

HENRYK SZERYNG AND SIMON RATTLE

"No one knows what music is. It is performed, listened to, composed, and talked about; but its essential reality is as little understood as that of its first cousin, electricity. We know that it detaches the understanding, enabling thoughts to turn inward upon themselves and clarify; we know that it releases the human spirit into some solitude of meditation where the creative process can freely act; we know that it can soothe pain, relieve anxiety, comfort distress, exhilarate health, confirm courage, inspire clear and bold thinking, ennoble the will, refine taste, uplift the heart, stimulate intellect, and do many another interesting and beautiful thing. And yet, when all is said and done, no one knows what music is. Perhaps the explanation is that music is the very stuff of creation itself."
LUCIEN PRICE

"I know that twelve notes in each octave and the varieties of rhythm offer me opportunities that all of human genius will never exhaust."
IGOR STRAVINSKY (1882 - 1971)

"What is music? This question occupied my mind for hours last night before I fell asleep. The very existence of music is wonderful, I might even say miraculous. Its domain is between thought and phenomena. Like a twilight mediator, it hovers between spirit and matter, related to both, yet differing from each. It is spirit, but it is spirit subject to the measurement of time. It is matter but it is matter that can dispense with space."
HEINRICH HEINE (1797 - 1856)

"To hear [Mozart's] music is to feel one has accomplished some good deed. It is difficult to say precisely wherein this good influence lies, but undoubtedly it is beneficial; the longer I live and the better I know him, the more I love music."
PYOTR ILYICH TCHAIKOVSKY,
in a letter to Nedejda von Meck

"Music is essentially useless, as life is."
GEORGE SANTAYANA (1863 - 1952)

BACH, SONATA No. 5

"Music stands quite alone. It is cut off from all the other arts.... It does not express a particular and definite joy, sorrow, anguish, horror, delight, or mood of peace, but joy, sorrow, anguish, horror, delight, peace of mind themselves, in the abstract, in their essential nature, without accessories, and therefore without their customary motives. Yet it enables us to grasp and share them fully in this quintessence."
ARTHUR SCHOPENHAUER (1788 - 1860)

"Music is the shorthand of emotion. Emotions which let themselves be described in words with such difficulty, are directly conveyed . . . in music, and in that is its power and significance."
LEO TOLSTOY (1828 - 1910)

"Music is the voice of all sorrow, all joy. It needs no translation."
HELEN EXLEY

JESSYE NORMAN

CLAUDIO ABBADO

"As a director, my definition of paradise would be to
be perpetually rehearsing Mozart's operas."
PETER HALL, b.1930

"I would walk ten leagues through the mud, the thing I
hate most in the world, to hear a good peformance of
Don Giovanni. If anybody quotes an Italian phrase out
of *Don Giovanni* immediately my tender memories of
the music recur to me and take possession of me...."
STENDHAL (1783 - 1842),
from *Life of Henri Brulard*

"Curran's favourite mode of meditation was with his
violin in his hand; for hours together would he forget
himself, running voluntaries over the strings, while his
imagination, collecting its tones, was opening all his
faculties for the coming emergency at the bar."
BENJAMIN DISRAELI (1804 -81)

"We listen to great music and know that all our joys and sorrows are part of something beyond our comprehension - and so infinitely valuable."
JESSE O'NEILL

"Loch Music
I listen as recorded Bach
Restates the rhythms of a loch.
Through blends of dusk and dragonflies
A music settles on my eyes
Until I hear the living moors,
Sunk stones and shadowed conifers
And what I hear is what I see,
A summer night's divinity."
DOUGLAS DUNN

BACH SONATA No. 5

BRITTEN PHANTASY, QUARTERLY ENDELLION

"All men must fear death, only the artist fears him not. He will move future generations when the bones of kings have long mouldered away. And secure in these convictions Mozart could stand there, when a thousand ears were listening for every quivering of a string, every whisper of a flute.... Be it fanatical enthusiasm, be it genuine human feeling: enough, at the moment I would rather have been Mozart than the Emperor Leopold."

ALEXANDER VON KLEIST, 1792,
from *Phantasien auf einer Reise nach Prag*

"The great geniuses suffer and must suffer, but they need not complain; they have known intoxication unknown to the rest of us and, if they have wept tears of sadness, they have poured tears of ineffable joy. That in itself is a heaven for which one never pays what it is worth."

CHARLES GOUNOD (1818 - 93)

"When I hear music, I fear no danger. I am invulnerable. I see no foe. I am related to the earliest times, and to the latest."

HENRY DAVID THOREAU (1817 - 62)

BRAHMS SONATA No. 2 in A Major

"Mozart makes you believe in God - much more than going to church - because it cannot be by chance that such a phenomenon arrives into this world and then passes after thirty-six years, leaving behind such an unbounded number of unparalleled masterpieces."
GEORG SOLTI, b.1912

There is an old Jewish legend about the origin of praise. After God created mankind, says the legend, He asked the angels what they thought of the world He had made. "Only one thing is lacking," they said. "It is the sound of praise to the Creator." So, the story continues, "God created music, the voice of birds, the whispering wind, the murmuring ocean, and planted melody in people's hearts."

"A Mozart Mass can make the unbeliever half believe."
JESSE O'NEILL

"Music, the greatest good that mortals know.
And all of heaven we have below."
JOSEPH ADDISON (1672 - 1719)
from *A Song for St. Cecilia's Day*

"I believe in God, Mozart and Beethoven."
RICHARD WAGNER (1813 - 83)

KYUNG WHA CHUNG

"When I hear a piece of music... I feel a delicious pleasure in which reason has no part. The habit of analysis comes afterwards to give birth to admiration. The emotion increasing in proportion to the energy or the grandeur of the ideas of the composer soon produces a strange agitation in the circulation of the blood; tears, which generally indicate the end of the paroxysm, often indicate only a progressive state of it, leading to something still more intense. In this case I have spasmodic contraction of the muscles, a trembling in all my limbs, a complete torpor of the feet and hands, a partial paralysis of the nerves of sight and hearing. I no longer hear, I scarcely hear - vertigo... a semi-swoon."
HECTOR BERLIOZ (1803 - 69)

"There is but one thing in the world that does me good, it is music; but it is a good that others would call agony. I wish I might hear ten times a day that air which tears me in pieces and brings back to me with ecstasy all that I regret."
JULIE-JEANNE-ELÉONORE DE LESPINASSE, 1774

"SOPRANOS"

"I am inclined to think that a hunt for folk songs is better than a manhunt of the heroes who are so highly extolled."
LUDWIG VAN BEETHOVEN (1770 - 1827)

"I grew up in a quiet spot and was saturated from earliest childhood with the wonderful beauty of Russian popular song. I am therefore passionately devoted to every expression of the Russian spirit.... As to this national element in my work, its affinity with folk songs in some of my melodies and harmonies comes from my early years in the country."
PYOTR ILYICH TCHAIKOVSKY (1840 - 93)

"The soul of a country is in its folk music. The country that has abandoned its folk music to commerce deserves a Coca Cola wake."
DR. MAYA V. PATEL

"The man that hath no music in himself,
Nor is not mov'd with concord of sweet sounds,
Is fit for treasons, stratagems, and spoils;
The motions of his spirit are dull as night,
And his affections dark as Erebus:
Let no such man be trusted."
WILLIAM SHAKESPEARE,
from *The Merchant of Venice*

"I always loved music; whoso has skill in this art is of a
good temperament, fitted for all things. We must teach
music in schools; a schoolmaster ought to have skill in
music, or I would not regard him; neither should we
ordain young men as preachers unless they have been
well exercised in music."
MARTIN LUTHER (1483 - 1546)

"Music is the voice that tells us that the human race is
greater than it knows."
MARION C. GARRETTY

DETAIL FROM "ARCHDUKE" BEAUX ARTS TRIO

"The infinite sinuousness, nuance, and complexity of music enable it to speak in a thousand different accents to a thousand different listeners, and to say with non-commital and moving intimacy what no language would acknowledge or express and what no situations in life could completely exhaust or make possible."
IRWIN EDMAN

"Where words leave off music begins."
HEINRICH HEINE (1797 - 1856)

"Music is the voice of all humanity, of whatever time or place. In its presence we are one."
CHARLOTTE GRAY, b.1937

"Music is the only language in which you cannot say a mean or sarcastic thing."
JOHN ERSKINE

SIR THOMAS BEECHAM

"The Prokofiev 'Romeo and Juliet' sends an entire audience om-pomming into the street, invisible swords flickering."
PAM BROWN

"Joy is more joyful, given a tune."
JANE SWAN, b. 1943

UNACCOMPANIED BASSOONIST

"In the Negro melodies of America I discover a great and noble school of music.... These beautiful and varied themes are the products of the soil. They are the folk songs of the United States. All the great musicians have borrowed from the songs of the common people.... I have myself gone to the simple tunes of the Bohemian peasants for hints in my most serious work....The Negro melodies are pathetic, tender, passionate, melancholy, solemn, religious, bold, merry, gay, gracious."
ANTONIN DVORAK (1841 - 1904)

DETAIL FROM MOZART CONCERTO FOR TWO PIANOS

DETAIL FROM BEETHOVEN SYMPHONIES

"Had Mozart (or for that matter Beethoven) been living today, I doubt very much whether he would have given us that wonderful flood of great music that he did. A genius like him would very soon have been seduced financially either by Hollywood to write film-music or by television to show off before millions or by the stage to write piffling musical comedies. This has happened to virtually every promising musical talent since Stravinsky, with the possible exception of Britten.
For this reason, I don't believe the world is ever going to see the likes of Bach or Mozart or Beethoven or Schubert or Brahms or Sibelius again, not of course that they happen very often anyway. We must be thankful for what we've got."
ROALD DAHL

"I've never heard such corny lyrics, such simpering sentimentality, such repetitious, uninspired melody. Man, we've got a hit on our hands!"
BRAD ANDERSON

SIR HENRY WOOD

"Before describing the emotions that this incomparable masterpiece stirred in me, I ask myself if any pen can ever translate them - but at least in such a way as to give some idea of what went on inside me during those unparalleled hours, the charm of which has dominated my life like a luminous apparition, a revelatory vision."

CHARLES-FRANÇOIS GOUNOD (1818 - 93),
from *Memoires d'un Artiste*

"Is it any weakness, pray, to be wrought on by exquisite music? To feel its wondrous harmonies searching the subtlest windings of your soul, the delicate fibres of life where no memory can penetrate, and binding together your whole being, past and present, in one unspeakable vibration; melting you in one moment with all the tenderness, all the love, that has been scattered through the toilsome years, concentrating in one emotion of heroic courage or resignation, all the hard-learned lessons of self-renouncing sympathy, blending your present joy with past sorrow, and your present sorrow with all your past joy?"

GEORGE ELIOT [Mary Ann Evans] (1819 - 80)

"As to the spiritual qualities of Mozart's music, the tempest-wind of his impetuous genius will never lack the power to sweep away the dreaming, contemplative spirits of this world, nor fill their world with sad and haunting visions. Sometimes the impact of his music is so immediate that the vision in the mind remains blurred and incomplete, while the *soul* seems to be directly invaded, drenched, as it were, in wave upon wave of melancholy."
STENDHAL (1784-1842),
from *Life of Rossini*

"After playing Chopin, I feel as if I had been weeping over sins that I had never committed, and mourning over tragedies that were not my own. Music always seems to me to produce that effect. It creates for one a past of which one has been ignorant and fills one with a sense of sorrows that have been hidden from one's tears."
OSCAR WILDE (1854 - 1900)

PAVAROTTI ▷

TCHAIKOVSKY VIOLIN CONCERTO, VICTORIA MULLOVA

" ...At the end, a Mozart symphony which delighted
me. My fatigue and the heat were excessive; but I had
an experience there which never happened to me before;
it was that the last piece seemed not only ravishing in
every respect but that, apparently, it caused my fatigue
to disappear while I was listening. That perfection,
that completeness, those delicate shadings, all that must
be the despair of musicians who have any soul
and any taste."

EUGÈNE DELACROIX (1798 - 1863),
from *Journals*

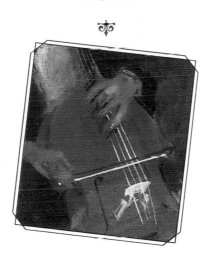

"There is something very wonderful in music. Words are wonderful enough; but music is even more wonderful. It speaks not to our thoughts as words do; it speaks straight to our hearts and spirits, to the very core and root of our souls. Music soothes us, stirs us up; it puts noble feelings in us; it melts us to tears, we know not how: - it is a language by itself, just as perfect, in its way, as speech, as words; just as divine, just as blessed...."
CHARLES KINGSLEY (1819 - 75)

"How is it that music can, without words, evoke our laughter, our tears, our highest aspiration?"
JANE SWAN, b.1943

"Music expresses that which cannot be said and on which it is impossible to be silent."
VICTOR HUGO (1802 - 85)

SIR ADRIAN BOULT

"Music may achieve the highest of all missions: she may be a bond between nations, races, and states, who are strangers to one another in many ways; she may unite what is disunited, and bring peace to what is hostile."
DR. MAX BENDINER

"Music binds us together with invisible threads."
PAM BROWN

"I have my own particular sorrows, loves, delights; and you have yours. But sorrow, gladness, yearning, hope, love, belong to all of us, in all times and in all places. Music is the only means whereby we feel these emotions in their universality."
H. A. OVERSTREET

"Music is the universal language of mankind."
HENRY WADSWORTH LONGFELLOW (1807 - 82)

"I go back to the G Minor Quintet for comfort, sometimes when I am most desperate. The kind of consolation it affords is parallel to what Wordsworth's poetry gives me - helping me to bear myself in the despair of solitude."
HAROLD BLOOM

"My son and I met days of depression together. We put on recordings of early, early blues, recorded by ancient men and women in the days of the hissing disc, put out the light and bayed at the moon in mournful accompaniment.
It always did the trick."
PAM BROWN, b.1928

"This music, so harmonious and so lofty in inspiration, so pure, both soft and sorrowful... made me forget as I listened to it my past woes and those that the future held perhaps in store for me."
ABBÉ MARTINANT DE PRÉNEUF, 1797

SIR MALCOLM SARGENT

"The pleasure of listening to delightful notes, with delightful words, uttered with taste and feeling by an accomplished and intellectual singer, is one of the most perfect that can fall to the lot of beings who are unable to hear the music of the spheres and the songs of Paradise."
ELIZA LESLIE

"The fine singer amazes. As the voice soars up we ask how this technique, this artistry is possible.
The great singer shows us only beauty.
We accept it as a gift."
MARION C. GARRETTY, b.1917

"Vaughan Williams knew there is no instrument in the world that possesses the loneliness and desolation that can be conveyed by the human voice."
CHARLOTTE GRAY

JESSYE NORMAN

DETAIL FROM AMADEUS QUARTET

"Music hath charms to soothe a savage breast,
To soften rocks, or bend a knotted oak."
WILLIAM CONGREVE (1670 - 1729)

†

"I felt raised above all care, all pain, all fear, and every taint of vulgarity was washed out of the world... That is wherein lies, for me, the moral power of music."
MARGARET FULLER (1871 - 1954)

†

"Music alone with sudden charms can bind
The wand'ring sense, and calm the troubled mind."
WILLIAM CONGREVE (1670 - 1729),
from *Hymn to Harmony*

†

"When I hear music, it seems to me that all the sins of my life pass slowly by me with veiled faces, lay their hands on my head, and say softly, 'My child.' "
SIDNEY LANIER

VICTORIA MULLOVA

"The Mozartian legacy, in brief, is as good an excuse for mankind's existence as we shall ever encounter and is perhaps, after all, a still small hope for our ultimate survival."
H. C. ROBBINS LANDON,
from *Mozart's Last Year*

"Bach opens a vista to the universe. After experiencing him, people feel there is meaning to life after all."
HELMUT WALCHA

DETAIL FROM JACQUELINE DU PRÉ MEMORIAL CONCERT

"Music speaks of Platonic truth - the ideal river rather than the polluted reality, love as we dream it rather
than we experience it, grief noble and uplifting rather than our distracted weeping. It is necessary to our survival and our sanity."
PAM BROWN

"I tell the story of love, the story of sorrow, the story that saves and the story that destroys.... I am the smoke which palls over the field of battle where men die with me on their lips.
I am close to the marriage altar, and when the grave opens I stand nearby. I call the wanderer home, I rescue the soul from the depths; I open the lips of lovers and through me the dead whisper to the living.
One I serve as I serve all, and the leaders I make my slaves as easily as I subject their slaves. I speak through the birds of the air, the insects of the field, the crash of waters on rock ribbed shores, the sighing of the winds in the trees and I am even heard by the soul that knows me in the clatter of the wheels on city streets."
ANONYMOUS

LEONARD BERNSTEIN ▷